Prisms of the Soul

Writings From a Sisterhood of Faith

Edited by Marcy Darin

MOREHOUSE PUBLISHING
Harrisburg, Pennsylvania

Prisms of the Soul

Copyright © The National Board of Episcopal Women 1996

Cover art © 1996 by Carol Bradbury Besheer

Morehouse Publishing

Editorial Office
871 Ethan Allen Hwy.
Ridgefield, CT 06877

Corporate Office
P.O. Box 1321
Harrisburg, PA 17105

Library of Congress Cataloging-in-Publication data:

Prisms of the soul : writings from a sisterhood of faith / edited by
    Marcy Darin.
            p.   cm.
        ISBN 0-8192-1676-3 (pbk.)
        1. Religious poetry, American. 2. American poetry—women authors.
    3. Meditations. 4. American poetry—20th century. I. Darin, Marcy
    PS595.R4P75   1996
    811'.54080382—dc20   96-27068
                                                                     CIP

ISBN: 0-8192-1676-3

Printed in the United States of America

Contents

Preface

Images of God

A Mother's Trinity 1
Reflections of Jesus 2
The Light of the World 3
Lilies 4
A Poem for Mary 5
Who Do You Say That I Am? 7
The Pool 8
At the Well 8
Reflections After Compline 9

Prayer

Prayer to the Triune God 12
Teresa Speaks to God 13
Morning Prayer 14
The Queen's Prayer 15
Sacred Dance 17
Given 18
The Holiness of Iona 18

Hope

I Know Your Resting Place 22
Collect for Silence 22
God is Near 23
The Season of Hope 25

Faith

Oh, Mary, Did You Know? 28

At the Feast in the Wilderness 29

God's Constant 30

The Crossing 30

Passages

Leaves of October...35

Ode to the Maiden...36

Sonnet 5...37

Redemption 39

Southern Awakening...40

Creativity

The Art of Spiritual Spring Cleaning.........................44

Surrender...45

The Moment 47

Work 48

Healing

Washington Beach 52

Oh Merciful God 54

Blind Woman 55

Worth the Pain 56

Sonnet 7...57

Another Ordinary Sunday 58

One Size Hugs All..59

Epiphany

I Sing In Celebration 62
Que Dios Les Beniga 64
To A Child of Faith..66
Epiphanies 67
Wheelies..69

Journey

The Circle 72
Letter to God 73
To The New Year 74
Yes, I Was There..75
The Stoning..76

Grief

To My Foster Son 80
Sonnet 11..81
Reflexiones de Una Madre, de Nombre Maria 83
Through Night Air 85
Life Goes On 87

Transformation

Fall 90
The Stranger..91
the new heaven 92
Eucharist 93
Chrysalis..93
A Woman's Burdens...94
Some Rambling Thoughts
On A Spring Afternoon 97

Witness

Mother Teresa 100

Love 101

@ Home 102

Spiritual Journey 103

New Life 105

Unity in Diversity 106

A Prayer for Beyond Beijing.............................. 107

The Girl at the Bus Stop 108

Seasons

Advent Visitation 112

Reflections on John the Baptist 113

The Annunciation of Our Lord 114

Hail, Mary 115

Nativity... 116

Christmas Transformation................................. 117

To Prepare 118

Ash Wednesday.. 118

The 8th Day of Lent, 1981 119

Holy Week.. 120

Of Lists and Lent... 121

Learning to Make Easter Bread......................... 122

Easter Vigil 123

Variation 2 123

Joy 124

Ascension.. 125

The Green Season.. 127

Collect and Reflection on All Saints' Day.......... 128

Communion of Saints... 129

All Saints 130

Preface

The meditations in this book, written by women throughout the Episcopal Church, are indeed, prisms of the soul. To each author, the image of God reflects a light ray of the Holy Mystery.

These prisms of the soul are like icons from which the light of Christ shines through the passages of life, in faith, joy, pain, sorrow, struggle, love, transformation, hope, grace, resurrection, and celebration.

Reading these meditations was, for me, like being on Holy Ground, knowing that each woman was touched by God to the innermost depth of her soul. These passages are truly sacramental: outward and visible signs of God's inward and invisible grace.

The offerings contained in this volume connect ray upon ray, a continuous spiritual, sacramental, and mystical oneness in the Body of Christ. As individual members of this one Body, the authors share a common story and vision which transcends time and space. It is a vision toward which all things are possible in God, dispersing an indelible light. Icons do that. Stories do that. Prisms of the Soul are just that. Our thanks to all of the women who have shared something of that holy light with us.

The Rev. Dr. Virginia M. Sheay
Executive Council Liaison to the
National Board of Episcopal Church Women

Images

Images of God

Evelyn Beatrice Longman Batchelder

A Mother's Trinity

Living God, the Three in One
Holy Spirit, Father, Son

We reflect His glory given
The Creator, the Protector, the sacrifice
On Earth as it is in Heaven.

Wind that blew across the sea
Creator who births galaxies and microbes
In whose joy All came to be.

Love's imperative is to "Create"
So we bear the children to complete our
  love
As did the Spirit boldly make.

Israel His presence knew
Protected from all the journey's tragedies
Always safe, the chosen few.

We protect those children borne
We shield with love, the only thing
possible
As the Father, evermore.

Infant in the manger laid
Sacrifice prepared from the moment of
His birth
For us descended to the grave.

Our sacrifice of flesh and blood
Children brought forth in agony, in
  trembling
As with the Son, are bathed in love.

Living God, the Three in One
Holy Spirit, Father, Son.

Jane E. Drichta
Del Rio, Texas

Reflections of Jesus

did Jesus ever look in a mirror
stand there and wonder
what the world saw?
did Jesus ever see his own face
in surprise
awed at the stranger staring back
the inadequate form given
to do a life's work
the features rendered so human
for carrying God?

Patricia R. Davis
Virginia Beach, Virginia

The Light of the World

New lilac leaves like small green tongues of flame,
translucent on the branches, fresh from bud,
hold all the light there is within the frame
my window makes. A wall as dull as mud
is backdrop: every leaf's a lucid flare
against this afternoon smudged charcoal grey.
The bishops, meeting earlier this year,
sought an image clearly to convey
"the Light of the World am I." Is it the burst
of glory when a switch defeats the night?
The radiance, when shadows are dispersed
from all a soul's dark caves by holy light?
   This tree stands, incandescently unfurled,
     an icon of the true Light of the World.

Christine Whittemore
Stroudsburg, Pennsylvania

The Light of the World

Lilies

Right about now, in parts of the world where this is springtime, the lilies are out in an incredible number of varieties and colors, some of which we associate with resurrection joy. God did a good job on all the flowers, but the lilies are a special blessing. They keep coming throughout the growing season, different strains at different times throughout the summer. A consistent hymn of praise to the goodness of God.

I can't think of a single reason why they should be so beautiful. To attract bees, people say, and I suppose it's true, but the bees would come anyway, drawn by smell of pollen. I think the lilies are beautiful simply because God loves to create beauty. The same reason you and I are beautiful in God's sight.

They are not uniform, the lilies. They are irregular. No two alike. But the irregularities are part of the beauty. They are what make lilies real. Just so with us: we are beautiful in our irregularities: our freckles, our hair that is curly when we wish it was straight, our laugh-lines, the bald spots we try to conceal. God must smile at our quibbles with how we look. We do not see how beautiful we are, but God does and goes on creating us in our astonishing diversity, just for the joy of it.

Barbara Cawthorne Crafton
New York, NY

Reprinted with permission of *Forward Movement Publications*

A Poem for Mary

Go singing, light-hearted, free,
Down to the silent sea.
Stars are fed by your delicate hand,
Angels weave through your hair.
Your eyes are lightning and summer's blue,
Yours a green footstep on the hill.
Morning celebrates your presence forever:
Here, now, everywhere
You are found in God's fullness. Avé!

Sue Stock
Greenville, Mississippi

Alison Vogel

Who Do You Say That I Am?

Foundation, guide, sword and healer: the quilt pictured here shows four metaphors for Jesus that speak powerfully to me.

At the bottom of the cross lie the foundation stones, reminding me that there are no spiritual shortcuts. Without a strong foundation, I am shaken by every tremor, toppled by every strong wind. Jesus Christ is the foundation to which I am learning to cling.

At the top of the cross soars a luminous white albatross. It is the albatross in C.S. Lewis' *Voyage of the Dawn Treader*, which symbolizes light, hope, guidance, help and compassion. Jesus Christ is the light that can pierce my darkness to lead me home.

At the right of the cross is a golden sword, reminding me of Jesus' saying in Matthew: "I have not come to bring peace, but a sword." Following Jesus can be painful, yet Jesus is the sharp sword that cuts off the dying part so the living part of me can be saved.

At the left of the cross is a hand, symbolizing healing. Jesus reaches out to touch and heal me, often through the hands of others. Jesus Christ is the one who can heal my body, mind and spirit.

There is balance, and conflict, in this scheme: the foundation, which anchors me, is in tension with the albatross, guiding me and encouraging me to soar. The sword that hurts is in tension with the hand that heals. Yet each is necessary and complements the other, connected in a circle that reflects the wholeness of Jesus.

Alison Vogel
Mercer Island, Washington

The Pool

I am a pool of light in the midst of a dark wood.
I am still but very deep.
Come to me
    plunge into my cool, green depths
and I will give you rest
    and the water of life
        and my peace, which passes all understanding.

Bonnie Harris-Reynolds
College Station, Texas

At The Well

"There cometh a woman of Samaria to draw water.
Jesus saith unto her, 'Give me to drink.'" John 4:7

I remember the water—
    cold/wet turned to light
        stones no longer dry.

You drank, spoke, drowned
    me to myself—forever
        distorted.
            Revealing.

Sally B. Sedgwick
Cincinnati, Ohio

Reflections After Compline

What we want is power,
What we get is frailty;
What we want is certainty,
What we get is ambiguity;
What we want is answers,
What we get is questions;
What we want is self-sufficiency,
What we get is interdependence;
What we want is permanence,
What we get is transience;
What we want is clarity,
What we get is mystery;
What we want is fantasy—
What we get is God.

Sue Stock
Greenville, Mississippi

Prayer

Prayer

Prayer to the Trinne God

Creator God
> For the great expanse of the universe,
> For this wondrous planet Earth,
> We give you thanks.

Redeemer God
> For the sacrifice of your self,
> For the saving power of love,
> We give you thanks.

Sustainer God
> For the prayers of saints and children,
> For the arts that lift our hearts,
> For the love of friends and family,
> We give you thanks and pray:

Enlighten our understanding,
Increase our faith,
Enlarge our hearts, O God,
Creator, Redeemer, Sustainer.

Sue Stock
Greenville, Mississippi

Teresa Speaks to God

How your love burns us
down and down, burns us
down like candles.

How your holy flame
eats our wicks, licks
and swallows our wax,

consumes us to brighten
and perfume the room.
How the fire follows

our threads, hungrily
devours our tallow,
burrows down through

the hearts of us
to the final flicker
into thin air, when

a curling filament of smoke
flowers from our charred ends
like incense, a prayer.

Luci Shaw
Menlo Park, California

13

Morning Prayer

Gracious God, as I awake,
let my first steps be in your footsteps,
that, throughout this day, I may think about
and pray for those less fortunate.

Help me remember that I am who I am
Because you gave your only Son
to die on the cross for me
not knowing my race, color or creed.

May I somehow help a person regardless
of who or what they are.
I ask this in the Name of your beloved Son
Our Lord and Savior Jesus Christ.

Esther H. Reynosa
San Antonio, Texas

The Queen's Prayer

Queen Liliuokalani was the last Hawaiian monarch and the only reigning queen of Hawaii. After her monarchy was dissolved in 1893, she was imprisoned for eight months in Iolani Palace. There she wrote many songs, including the beautiful "Ke Aloha O Ka Haku," better known as The Queen's Prayer. In 1896, she was baptized and confirmed at St. Andrew's Episcopal Cathedral, later serving as choir director and first organist at Kawaiahao Church. Although her legal name was changed to Lydia Dominis, to her people she remained Queen Liliuokalani, who did much to improve the quality of their lives. She died in 1917 and was interred in the Royal Mausoleum in Honolulu.

O kou aloha no
A ia i ka lani
A o kou oia io
He hemolele loi.

O Lord thy loving mercy
high as the heavens
tells us of thy truth
And 'tis filled with holiness.

Kou noho mihi ana
O paa haoia
O oe kuu lama
Kou nani kou koo

Whilst humbly meditating
Within these walls imprisoned
Thou art my light my haven
Thy glory my support.

Mai nana ino ino
Na hewa o kanaka
A ka e hui kala
A mae mae no.

O look not on their failings
Nor on the sins of men
Forgive with loving kindness
That we might be made pure.

No lai la e ka Haku
Ma la lo kou e heu
Ko makou maluhia
A mau loa aku no. Amene

For thy grace I beseech thee
Bring us 'neath thy protection
And peace will be our portion
Now and forever more. Amen.

Geri Tom
Honolulu, Hawaii

Dorothy McLean

Sacred Dance

"And Miriam the prophetess... took a timbrel in her hand; and all the women went out after her with timbrels and with dances." Exodus 15:20

A group of women meets monthly in my church's parish hall for "sacred dance." We laugh that some people wouldn't recognize what we do as either sacred or dance. But whether our movements are wild with drums and didgeridoos, sassy with jazz, pensive with the blues, or joyful with traditional chorales, we know them as both.

After warming up, we reflect on a psalm or other text, each of us finding a special image or phrase and discovering from some speechless inner place a gesture or two to embody it. Then we teach each other our movements. In a circle—often surrounded by candles and scarves—we dance.

What happens is always different, surprising and beautiful. Filled with a grace that is oblivious to shape or size, skill or expertise—all those things highly valued by our culture—we dance in joy and pain, hope and fear, longing and blessing.

I dance at home, too. Just out of the shower. Or crossing the room to answer a phone. Or when I take a break from reading student papers. Sometimes my arms and legs match what I want to pray: kneeling to scoop up a situation, standing to embrace someone in grief. When I don't know how to pray, I dance—arms and legs, breath and belly, trusting God both to lead and understand my gestures.

Angier Brock
Bon Air, Virginia

Given

(Reflections after a workshop on prayer with Madeleine L'Engle)

God is. I am. Prayer is. Amen.

Penny Reid
Seattle, Washington

The Holiness of Iona

"...where two or three are gathered..."

To Madeleine L'Engle and Barbara Braver,
companions in pilgrimage

Westward across Mull along the single track,
between violet hills and under the torn cloth of
clouds. Finally over the brief channel from
Fionnphort, the green-gray waves chipping away at
the hull of the ferry, with the buffet of sea-wind

rough as the breath of God. Pilgrims, we can hardly wait to inhale the holy island's scent of sanctity.

Once here, the sea between the rocks lies tranquil, clear as green glass over the white sand. Cottage gardens cluster beyond the jetty, vivid with delphiniums, rank with nasturtiums. But scores of day-trippers, with their backpacks and bikes, crowd the asphalt path to the Abbey; tourists, lacing the air with unrecognized syllables, fill the craft shops (local pottery, Celtic jewelry), and the Abbey gift shop (bookmarks, key rings, postcards).

Expecting to find Columcille, and Patrick—the ancient saints blessing us with solitude, with a peace that drops like fading light behind the hills—all we sense is... an absence. Among the shrines, crosses, gravestones, a nunnery, we each say how much we miss it—like the wild gold of the iris whose dark summer leaves hug the creases of the island, their spring boldness faded to a single wilted rag here, there.

On the last day, a walk together across the backbone of rock to a bay pebbly as Galilee, a meal of fish and soda bread, evening prayer in the small cell of a guest room show us where to look: Though our high anticipation detoured us, now, when we least expect it, here it is, God's felt presence in our human trinity of longing.

Luci Shaw
Menlo Park, California

19

Hope

I Know Your Resting Place

Like sharp white feathers,
Scruffy clouds scrape across
the intensely blue sky, dropping
Chunks of blue onto our milky
Winter skin, mottling our
Pale flesh with vivid color.

From beyond the sky, that
We can see, and the heaven we
Can believe, a gleaming silver
Wing flashes, sending forth
A signal—that death has no
Finality, and life endures
Forever.

Betsy R. Slyker
Fredericksburg, Texas

Collect for Silence

Most Holy Spirit, who graces us with whispered voice, still us into Your quiet.
When our voices cease their clamor, Yours may be heard
and Your presence may resound... as mute Hosannas in our silence:
through God our Mother, whose hushing finger stills our trembling lips.

Amen.

Diane Moore
Littleton, Colorado

God is Near

When you feel sad and lonely
And you think no one cares,
Look into the heavens—
God is always there.
He sees our every ache and pain
And all our troubled thoughts;
Tell him who knows you well
The battles you have fought.
Lift your thoughts and smile again,
You have nothing else to fear;
God will listen and pray with you
And will forever and ever be near.

Kelly Rhode Kuennen
St. Louis, Missouri

Kathryn Bradshaw

The Season of Hope

"I will restore to you the years that the locust hath eaten..." Joel 3:25

A few years ago I awoke to a living nightmare. Within six months, my husband was downsized out of a job; we were forced to move from the home where we'd raised our four children; my 23-year-old son was paralyzed in a construction accident; my teen-aged daughter and I were estranged; and I was in menopause with heart palpitations and hot flashes. I did not have long to wait before the locusts devoured my last shreds of hope.

Most of my life had been lived in hopeful anticipation: I marched onward and upward toward the next school year, next season, next job. Even though I would sometimes encounter a rocky path, I still looked toward a good outcome. Yet with a husband out of work, my children hurt, and lingering depression, life seemed hopeless.

A prayer group offered support. I read voraciously from the Bible, inspirational works and self-help books. But nothing quite eased the pain or emptiness; I felt the drought of Thomas Merton's "desert time."

Several years passed; gradually I eased into a new life. My husband retired, and we retreated to a small cabin overlooking our favorite lake where our daughter and her husband live with us. We are learning how to integrate our lives with love. Our son wears a leg brace and manages quite well with crutches. When he married his rehabilitation nurse, the entire family cried with happiness. Time and medication helped me die to my old self so that a new woman could be born. I felt different, refreshed, renewed: my locust-devoured years were being restored.

Marianne Merrill Moates
Sylacavage, Alabama

Faith

Faith

Oh, Mary, Did You Know?

Mary: Virgin, teenage maiden.
>Ready to bloom, at the age of ripening.
>Innocent. Trusting. Expectant.
>You were a receptive vessel for conception.
>Did you know what awaited you on the other side of your mystical
>experience?

Mary: Mother.
>Your body opened to bring a unique life into
>this world.
>You suckled him at your breast.
>As he grew to manhood, did you know joy
>and pride?
>Did you expect the pain and sorrow which
>awaited you on the other side of his life?

Mary: Old Woman of Wisdom. Crone.
>Oh, the agony and pain you must have felt
>as you watched your son die on the cross.
>Did you know what awaited you on the other side of the cross?

God did not let hope die.
Your son is alive. In some mysterious way,
He lives in *us*. Hope Love Wisdom Live.

Judith Yeakel
Langley, Washington

At The Feast in the Wilderness

Even as a grain of sand
  on the desert wind,
Even as the smallest fragment
  of dirt
Have I been carried on a mighty wind.

Even as a creature
  have I crawled.
Even as a rodent
  have I felt cold shadows
  of the flight of creatures
  greater than I.
Even in fear
  have I deceived
  the eyes of circling vultures.

Helpless
  have I seen the wind
  swallow my voice.
Alone
  have I stood at the abyss.
Trembling
  have I known that
This is holy.

And
Even as a grateful saint,
Even as a child of light created
With joy
have I sung
With joy
of my Lord
Who answers every crying in the wind.

Sandra Willey
Colorado Springs, Colorado

God's Constant

God's constant:
this promise of
His love that never ends or fails.

As light spun out of darkness
so came Love,
complete, entire, encircling
time and earth
that each of us might see the way
to enter Him,
and come at last
alive.

I Corinthians 13

Eleanor Smith
Tulsa, Oklahoma

The Crossing

As we were crosssing the Albemarle Sound in the early morning fog—with one mile visibility—it occurred to me that this crossing was like living with faith. From our thirty-foot Pearson sailboat, neither land nor channel marker could be seen. We checked our Inland Waterway chart and followed our compass, heading north. With faith we searched for the markers to lead us to our destination, avoiding the shoals as we progressed from one marker to another, keeping the green marker on our starboard and the red on our port side. Yet there were moments when we could see nothing, and we held our breaths until someone would yell "I see it!" Relieved, we knew we were still on course and making headway.

Life is often like that. We struggle along, knocked about by choppy waters, difficult situations, family stress—maybe held in foglike bondage. We look intently for a sign to ease our minds, lessen our anxiety. A moving Eucharist, a beautiful sunset, a new friend, a child's joy, give us an awareness of God's presence, serving as signs that our life is "on course."

Gwynn Kelley
Wilton, Connecticut

Como atravesábamos la Sonda de Albemarle en un barco de velas Pearson de 30 pies, por la mañana temprano, de un diá neblinoso, se me ocurrío que este pasaje fue como vivir la vida con fe: no se veía la tierra, ni aún un marcador de navegación. Revisamos nuestra carta de navegación de la Inland Waterway, y seguíamos nuestra rosa de vientos, dando a la dirección correcta—al norte—y con fe buscábamos los marcadores para guiarnos a nuestra destinación, evitando los bajíos, progresando de un marcador a otro, manteniendo los marcadores verdes a la mano estribor, y los rojos a la mano babor. A veces no podíamos ver nada por varios minutos. Buscábamos atentamente el marcador en el horizonte—un señal. Alguíen exclamaría—¡Lo veo!—Aliviados, sabíamos que estuvimos todavía en el rumbo, y progresando. La vida a menudo es así. Nuestro camino es una lucha, bofetados por las aguas agitadas: situaciones difíciles, presiones familiales, tal ves prisioneros en una cautividad espiritual neblinosa. Nos preguntamos si estamos ya en curso, si hemos progresado, o ¿nos hemos estraviado? y buscamos atentamente un señal para aliviar nuestras mentes, para sosegar nuestra ansiedad. Una Eucaristía emocionante, una hermosa puesta del sol, un nuevo amigo, el gozo de un niño, haciéndonos conscientes de la presencia de Dios—estos, y muchos mãs, nos sirven de señales que nuestra vida está "en rumbo."

Gwynn de Kelley
Wilton, Connecticut

Passages

Kathryn Bradshaw

Leaves

Leaves of October

The Falling Leaf Moon hangs in the sky, but the Moon of the Long Night
    is near.
As chloroplasts die each green mask fades, exposing colors
    of pending demise.
When breezes break the leaf stalk's bond, broad blades glide or spiral
    in final descent.
Then each leaf reposes as ordained, one flat, some hunched,
    many wounded or curled.
Below me, the Brandywine River in reflected light, catches a landscape brushed
    by the sun.
From the opposite shore a woodpecker drums, naming beech bronze, maple scarlet
    and more.
Down stream from the rapids where the river runs wide, an exodus comes
    into view.
Painted leaves journeying on the skin of water pass by like the "Sioux Nation"
    in final retreat.
Little bands, streaming columns, a mottled lot, all destined to die as they drift
    to the sea.

Bobbett A. Mason
Wilmington, Delaware

Ode to the Maiden

Ode to the maiden as she sits down to play;
  her fingers grope on the keys,
    unused to the black and white places.
She struggles to learn, to grow, to develop,
  to master life on the piano,
    to become skilled on its keys.

Ode to the matron as she sits down to play;
  her fingers move with assurance
    from years of practice, experience, and growth.
The music she plays tells a story
  of a life lived in the symphony of family,
    of relationships, of work.

Ode to the wise woman as she sits down to play;
    this time not on the piano,
  but on the resonating harpsichord.
For now this wise woman has come into her own,
  has expanded beyond her previously held limits:
  she is free, free at last, to be and to soar.

Isle of Iona
June 1994

Elizabeth Davies
Bellevue, Washington

Sonnet 5

Child and old woman, here again I sit,
Adolescent, mother, yet I'm still
Presiding at the table, candles lit,
Widow and wife I am. The plates I fill
With food set out at places freshly laid
Are honoring with love each coming guest.
How many are the meals that I have made
Night after night, nor can find the best?
I'll keep the laughter and the sad shed tears,
Would give none up; one lost would make me less.
Add all in all, the ecstasies, the fears:
Together they redeem, restore, redress.
I light the candles, bless the food, and you
Who grace the table make the myth come true.

Madeleine L'Engle
New York City

Alison Vogel

Redemption

Redemption

My feet are ugly.
I hate my feet.
My feet are big and bony and crooked.
Shoes don't fit.

When I was a little girl, I had little girl
   feet.
Soft and small and straight and true.
Dancing, hopping, skipping, and fleet.
Chasing, climbing, stomping, swinging
   high.
That little girl's daddy loved her too much,
   loved her all wrong.
He tried to put her in a box so she
   wouldn't grow up to be someone else's
   love.
He put her body and heart and mind into
   a box.
But she had to grow.
And when there wasn't room some things
   got bent.

My feet ache sometimes.
I use my feet a lot.

My feet are different than my daughter's
   feet.
We like to compare.

My little girls have perfect little girl feet.
Soft and small and straight and true.
Running, teasing, tickling and fast.
Twirling, leaping, jumping over mud
   puddles.
I love my little girls.
Too much ever, ever to put them in a box.
They really belong to God, you know,
   and I just get to help them grow up
   for a while.
Big and strong and straight and true.

My feet are getting old.
Inside, I still have little girl feet.
I love those little girl feet.
I can love my feet.
My feet are beautiful.

Alison Vogel
Mercer Island, Washington

Southern Awakening

I was raised a Southern Belle, she spoke
in gentle words, so soft a voice,
and God made man to care for me
to think my thoughts
speak my words
so I could be a lady, free,
unhampered by the devious world
of making decisions, living my life.

At forty-six I learned, she spoke
in a firm, still-gentle woman's voice,
in God's image we were made
both man and womankind,
and man, not God, set limits
on my life. Don't quote Paul to me.
Did Paul tell Lydia, dealer
in purple cloth to royalty,

"Go home to your family.
Give up this crazy idea of being
a businesswoman?"

No. He baptized Lydia, broke bread,
and blessed her household. Paul knew.
God knew that women
had work to do. Brains and plans
and prayers too big to conceal
in white kid gloves and picture hats.

Lois Oller Nasados
Longview, Texas

reprinted with permission from St. Mary's Press

Creativity

The Art of Spiritual Spring Cleaning

I have never really enjoyed washing windows, but I recently discovered a way to make this task more satisfying.

While you are washing, reflect upon the windows of your soul—your eyes. Whether your vision is 20/20 or can you barely see, the spiritual importance lies in what you look at and how you respond to it. Which books do you read? What television programs and movies do you watch? If Jesus were sitting next to you, would it make a difference?

In the story of the Good Samaritan, both the priest and the Levite "saw" the man in distress by the roadside, but their hearts were not affected enough for them to act.

Do you witness pain and feel compassion, and then do whatever you can to help?

Co-mingled with all the sadness around us is an abundance of beauty. Do you see it and give thanks, or take it for granted?

When the windows in my house are clean, I can see better. How I act upon what I see speaks volumes about whether or not I am a woman after God's own heart.

Kathryn Libby
Branford, Connecticut

Surrender

embrace
the silence
listen to
the still
small voice
within
reach out
and grasp
the sudden
inspiration
lest it
float away
like a
curled leaf
in the wind.

Dorothy Lauer
Redmond, Washington

Erin Wells

The Moment

"Be still and know that I am God."   Psalm 46:10

If you could know
  That all the time
The world would ever have
  Is in the moment now
  In which you stand,
    That in your hand
    The future's bent
  And all the promise
  Of the past's intent
  Is held, would you not
Wait and listen and be still?
  Would you not let such mystery
Poured from unimagined source
  Fill and fill and finally overflow
  The moment, until you, a living
    Fragment of eternity,
  Hear its measured beat
    And take its tempo
For your heart and hands and feet?

Ann Sweetser Watson
Marion, Massachusetts

Work

After the angel spoke
first to her in light
then to him in dreams, he knew
something was wrong yet wonderful.

His work was to cut out
and pound together tables
benches and chests but her chair
changed beneath his hands. Pegs
burgeoned into centers of lilies
arm rests formed apples. Dawn
and twilight followed her down
terraced paths and inside
luminous scent
of wilderness rain filled him.
Palm trees grew
around table legs. Wheat bundled
and grapes clustered in cedar.

In Bethlehem and Egypt
olive, acacia, cypress swirled
until once again an angel came
called them home to Nazareth
and light, always light
centered on one at his side
a child who rubbed warmth into
and tiredness out of hands.

It was last visit angel flames
that helped the old man understand
with sudden seeing
reflected light that forces
leaf and bud from kiln-dried wood.

Patricia Flower Vermillion
Hampton, Virginia

Healing

Washington Beach

I hear waves crash against the rocks near me,
   but I feel safe and sheltered under trees.
I see Sea gulls and Blue Herons fly above me
   and cover my shadow as they settle on the long
   tree branch.

I feel goosebumps trickle down my back as the
   storm comes,
   but I don't care because I am warm and secure.
I smell the salt from the ocean as the waves come
   closer and closer to me and the tree branches
   get tighter and tighter.

I watch as the storm comes closer and
   the waves reach out to touch my cold bare feet.
I hear the Sea gulls screech above me,
   they give me company since I am out by myself
   on Washington Beach.

I feel the harsh wind blow against my face,
   I rub my hands to get warm and run farther into
   the woods.

Dorothy McLean

I see a waterfall crashing against the freezing cold
    rocks.
    I sit and watch as the tree seems to clutch me.

I hear the black clouds swirl and swirl around,
    I feel sheltered as I walk behind the waterfall as
        water trickles down my arms.
I feel safe behind the water where it's barely damp.

I look at all the trees around me,
    as I stand a branch scratches my cold wet back.
I look up into the sky and notice a Sea gull and a
    Blue Heron flying above.
The day is bright and has fluffy white clouds.
    I know the storm is over; I walk back to the
        beach.

It is very peaceful now, very peaceful.
    Someday I wish the world would be like this.

Katherine Larsen, Age 10
Austin, Texas

Oh Merciful God

Oh merciful God, my nights are long.
   Chaos fills my spirit
I have lost the sense of your loving presence.
   I have lost the strength of your firm guidance.
My thoughts scuttle like dry leaves before the
winds.
   Or they are caught in swirling clouds and have
      no form or purpose.

My flesh is weary.
   My songs are muted.
A darkness possesses me.
   O God, bring me into your center.
Fill me again with light, zeal and purpose.
   Enfold me in your peace.
Enable me to show forth your glory, your strength
   and your love.
Lord have mercy.

Anonymous (member of the Church of the
Epiphany Kerygma Bible study group)
Danville, Virginia

Blind Woman

Blind Woman

A blind woman follows the cross.
Not the gold one, laced
long round her throat,
but the one made of light,
thousands of lights floating
white as a baby's milk teeth.
Enough for a blind woman to see.

Carol Bradbury Besheer
Bellevue, Washington

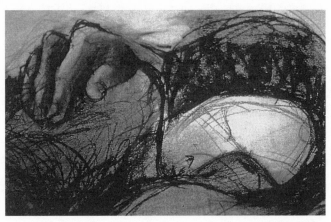

Carol Bradbury Besheer

Worth the Pain

Any mother will tell you: the last month of waiting for a baby seems to last forever. Time crawls slowly up until the due date. After the magic day comes and goes, and there is still no baby, time stands still! Those long days are full of dreamy hopes and vague fears. Most of all, they are full of expectant curiosity and longing to see and hold the baby which has been awaited for so long.

"Just let it be healthy," expectant parents pray as the time draws near. Life looks perilous when one thinks about the tiny being soon to embark upon it. Life is hard. It can be painful. There are so many things, parents think anxiously, that can happen to my baby.

Mary must have had all of those thoughts. This young mother would soon see her son die before her, surely the most unnatural pain a parent can know. The fulfillment of the primary desire of all mothers and fathers, to protect their children from harm, was not granted to Mary.

Parents who have lost children are sometimes asked if they would rather not have been parents in the first place than to experience the terrible pain. Is it really better to have loved and lost, as the poet said, than never to have loved at all? Yes, it was worth all the pain of my loss to have had my child for as long as I did, they say. The gift of a child was not something they would have given up, no matter what happened later. I suppose Mary would have answered the same way.

Barbara Cawthorne Crafton
New York, NY

Reprinted with permission of *Forward Movement Publications*

Sonnet 7

"It is not good for man to be alone," said God.
So God made two to be forever one,
And failed. Formed from dust and lowly sod
The two could not leave well enough alone.
They turned from God and ate forbidden fruit,
So God exiled them from their birthright home.
They knew each other, then. The point is moot.
Lost, hungry, they were forced to roam
The world of spirit more than that of earth.
They knew each other, then, the pain of love
That made two one, and was the cause of birth.
How strangely wise of God to make them move.
Only by breaking and mending can we be
The unique one, by God's wild love set free.

Madeleine L'Engle
New York City

57

Another Ordinary Sunday

I greeted Homecoming Sunday nursing a cold and determined—this time—to take care of myself, too (novel thought for a mother). For me, that meant letting my husband, Rob, take full responsibility for the troops (Clarke, 7, and Carolina, 3) and dancing the fine line of laying low while being fully present.

First, by God's grace, I chose to sit in the car alone while Rob dropped the kids at Choristers and nursery before heading to choir. The unanticipated blessing for me was quietly sitting in the back of our van, behind smoky windows, watching the body of Christ arrive. Gathering belongings. Maneuvering youngsters. The arrival show was so perfectly choreographed—no one seemed to miss a beat. During what I know personally to be a potentially frantic few minutes, I watched as my friends came forward: to worship, teach Sunday School, socialize, serve and finally, to rest and renew.

In those moments I was filled with such warmth—a respect and admiration that I recognized as a healing balm for me. Then when I joined in the service that assurance grew: the children sang first, a new acolyte did his part beautifully, a crowd of able (again by God's grace) teachers were commissioned, all complete with a visit from George, our parish's lay minister who happens to be a puppet.

Clearly, God took an "Ordinary" Sunday and miraculously healed me, body and spirit, among His own.

Penny Reid
Seattle, Washington

One Size Hugs All

Old or young or long or short
Or plump or thin, it's clear
All arms are just exactly right
for hugging someone dear!

Bonnie Compton Hanson
Santa Ana, California

Epiphany

I Sing in Celebration

How could I not celebrate
   the presence of our God
in the twinkle of a falling leaf
   that lights upon my path,
in a bush aflame with berries red
   that signals me to stop,
in the spiral of a red-tailed hawk
   that hovers overhead?

How could I not celebrate
   the presence of our God
in the joyful kiss of Springtime
   after Winter's monologue,
in a mother's all embracing love
   for tender infant flesh,
in the fingers intertwining
   of two rough and wrinkled hands?

How could I not celebrate
   the presence of our God
in one who came to show us love
   and teach us how to live,

in eyes that wept and hands that healed,
   and wounds that bled like ours,
in death that brought us freedom
   and broke the bonds of time?

I sing in celebration
   to our co-creator God
who dwells in all creation
   from the yew tree to the lamb,
who plants in us the seeds of love
   and prunes away the fear,
who feeds us with amazing grace
   and hears our every prayer.

Wendy von Oech
Atherton, California

Que Dios Les Beniga

As I was walking out the door
Jesus Christ
came up to me and asked, slowly,
"Does anyone here
speak Spanish?"

"Si, yo hablo,"
"Yes, I speak," I said.

He was short and unshaven, and also had
a thin wife,
standing by,
never saying
a word.

"We are from Guatemala, see."
He showed me a bus ticket.
"We came from Tuscon."
(He pronounced the "c.")
"Mi hermano está en Massachusetts."
"My brother is in Massachusetts."
"I have friends in New Jersey.
But we have no money, no food.
Her sister (he pointed, not trusting my Spanish),
her sister can send money, a little money
from California.
But someone must come to Western Union
with identification."

"No es mi iglesia."
"This is not my church."
"I live 50 miles from here.
Let me find someone
who can help."

"The Lord is here," I told them.
"They need someone to take them
to Western Union."

Returning, I found them sitting in chairs,
two chairs scattered in the large room.
"You may move the chairs and sit together," I said.

We gave them food, and
my friends said to wait for a church employee
to help them.

Leaving for home, I said,
"Que Dios les beniga."
"God bless you..."
and should have asked for their blessing
instead.

Anne L. Haehl
Lawrence, Kansas

To A Child of Faith

You'll never be sure
On what right path
Your feet should follow,
But you'll know.

And perhaps Faith's finest test
Is whether we can put our lives
In congruence
With what we know.

For surety, by its own definition
can only be a part of
Some cold, quantified and comfortable world
That isn't yours, or mine.

And rightly so.

Joyce Cleave Gibb
Ellenburg, Washington

Epiphanies

In a small boy's answering hug
I touched thy hem, O Lord.
In the loving wonder in his eyes
I got a glimpse of thee.

In the rich striving of weeds
Pushing sturdily through the verdant grass,
I see my sins, O Lord,
Lustily destroying what is good
In the garden of my life.
And as I pull them, root and branch
From their grasping clutch in the warm, moist
earth;
I see thy loving hand,
Gently, and not so gently,
Weeding my garden of life.

In the breaking of the Bread,
In the pouring of the Wine,
In the understanding glance of a friend,
In the self-revealing judgment of a foe;
I see Thee, Lord Jesus, I see thy plan;
And I see that it is good;
And it is enough for me, O Lord.

Joan R. Sheldon
Lacey, Washington

Whee

Wheelies

Stepping out to beat the sun before it set, I heard a little boy—he looked to be about four years old—call out to ask where I was going. As he pedaled vigorously toward me on his tiny bike, I knelt down to answer, seeking a fitting word for exercise. Sighing, he replied, "I don't know how to exercise. I'll ask my momma."

Then he took off in wide circles, calling, "Watch me." On each round—at the same place—he managed to pull the front wheel an inch above the pavement, his arms struggling to pull the handlebars upward as he shouted, "Did you see? Did you see?"

"Yes, you're doing great," I said in praise. Forgetting the impending sunset, my heart centered on meeting this little boy's needs. His tiny wheelies made me laugh inside—he was so pleased with his accomplishments. Someone called, he rushed home.

Continuing to honor the precious moment lifted my spirit, creating a new song in my heart. His trust and joy in me was so special. We had stopped to delight in wheelies, and ended up delighting in God and God in us. Often little things bless us, leaving special memories to ponder as we see God's handiwork in our experiences—even in little boys' wheelies.

Ione Grable
Orlando, Florida

Journey

Journey

The Circle

Cautiously pathing
Their yet concealed differences,
Two people approached
Each other in circles
Stepped out with the plan
of avoiding the other's
Potential threat;
But as they proceeded
To continue circling,
Passing according to
Chosen circumferences,
It was discovered that,
Despite their effort,
The course that they followed
Had become concentric,
So that in one instant
Of total sensation
To body and spirit together,
They touched.

Patti Dewing
Rolla, Missouri

Letter to God

Dear God,
Let me,
the daughter who chose apocryphal St. Veronica
for a cloth that glowed your face,
Learn to cherish the bloodstains of Saturday's laundry.
Let me bake bread knowing full well
angels will not keep it from burning.
Let me scrub the lasagna dish while
friends chatter in the living room,
and no gentle stranger comes to bid me oil his feet.
Remind the daughter who ached to be your mystic
that for her, the ordinary
takes more courage.

Jeannette Cooperman
St. Louis, Missouri

To The New Year

You are a blank sheet
As yet not stained by evil
By cruelty and selfishness
And endless strife
Committed by us all
Who move on planet Earth.

Yet we know well
That moments after you are born
The soiling will commence;
The blood of a thousand souls
Will stain your purity.
For we, possessed by power
Far beyond our strength
By longing for material things
Enthralled yet petrified
By concepts we can hardly understand
And prejudiced by feelings
Of exaggerated power and importance
Fail to be receptive
To the gifts of Grace Divine.

How can we, so captivated,
So enchanted by our willfulness
Admit with grace and due humility
That it is God who is in charge?
Who sets us on our way.

So let us confidently
And with hopeful hearts
Inscribe the pages of your youth
With love, with caring and compassion
For one another, near and far.

New Year's Day, 1994

E. Anne Kramer
Southfield, Michigan

Yes, I Was There

Glancing at the church bulletin, I recognized the hymn as my favorite, its plaintive verse like a silver thread woven into my memory. I had returned from a recent trip to Israel filled with the memory of rich physical and spiritual experiences.

"Were you there when they pierced him in the side?" I was brought back to the narrow, crowded path on the cobblestoned streets of Old Jerusalem. When a fellow traveler had remarked that the streets probably looked the same when Jesus carried his cross, I suddenly realized that I was stepping on the very stones Jesus did. I felt strong compassion for God's son as he painfully fulfilled his destiny. For what? For me! Yes, I was there when they pierced him in the side.

"Were you there when they laid him in the tomb?" Entering the sacred tomb, I had placed my palm against the cold damp cave walls and felt the stark contrast between stone and flesh. I recalled that Pontius Pilate had ordered his "high tech" boulder placed over the tomb's opening, yet the world would shout for 2,000 years: "He is risen!"

"Oh sometimes it causes me to tremble..." Thankful for God's gift of insight, I tearfully affirmed, "Yes I have seen! I was there! Yes, I believe!"

Orrene Raby
Oshkosh, Wisconsin

75

The Stoning

The rocks were piled
At the roadside with care;
The target, the harlot who
Soon would be there.
The men were seething
And hot with a plot
To test whether Jesus
Obeyed Torah—or not.
The woman who sinned
Was part of the plan.
She was brought out forthwith—
But where was the man?

Stoning to punish,
Say what you will;
The object, of course,
To maim and to kill.
No judges here
Nor even a jury,
A lone woman sinner
To face mounting fury.
Search for a clue
As much as you can,

No reference is made
To the adulterous man.

But Jesus was there
With justice at hand.
He knelt there before them
And wrote in the sand.
He knelt there in sorrow,
Brave and alone,
Said, "He without sin
Might cast the first stone."

Well, there's no one among us
With conscience so clear
We feel we could face Jesus
With nothing to fear.
We've told this story
The best that we can;
The woman was saved—
But who was the man?

Evelyn Whitenack Shedd
Woodridge, New Jersey

Grief

To My Foster Son

This Is Not Jacob's Story

I wrestled with you
not by the waters at Penniel
But in my living
room, as you kicked the piano
and ripped apart
my books.

I wrestled with you
in your room
where you tore
a hole in the wall.

I wrestled with you at the motel
where you screamed your rage
and I could not calm you.

You put out not my thigh
but my shoulder
which even now
aches in the morning.

What message did you bring
that I, a fool,
missed as I let you go
without your blessing me?

Anne L. Haehl
Lawrence, Kansas

Sonnet 11

God! The world is so big, our tiny lives so small,
How can we believe that our love matters?
Death has torn all I care for to terrible tatters.
Did our love matter? Oh, God, does it matter at all?
Countless galaxies swirl in the alien spaces,
Great furnaces of raging nuclear power
Against whose blasts the comets swiftly shower
Reflecting heaven on our human faces.
Life and death are hardly held apart
And yet this one death's impact is so great
The breathing of the universe must wait
Upon the ceasing of this single heart.
Dear love, if what I feel now is not true,
God never was, not God, not I, not you.

Madeleine L'Engle
New York City

Carol Bradbury Besheer

Reflexiones de Una Madre, de Nombre Maria

Divinos desvelos produce tu llanto,
tus primeros dientes, tus primeros pasos,
tu primera fiebre, primer abrazo.
Crece mi niño, crece fuerte,
crece mi tesoro que yo velo... crece,
refúgiate en mi regazo, apoya en mi pecho tu frente.
Aquí estoy para acariciarte,
en cerco de amor protegerte.
No temas, niño bonito, no temas mi niño... crece.

Treinta primaveras han pasado y
arrullarte quiero de nuevo, cuando cansado,
con hambre y frío, buscas lugar de reposo,
buscas refugio y cariño.
Porque aunque eres Dios eres hombre;
aunque eres Dios eres mi Hijo.
Y quiero enjugar tu llanto, sacudirte
el polvo del camino y arroparte con mi rebozo
como cuando eras chico.

De lejos sigo tus pasos,
y mi corazón se estremece ante la burla y
el desafió, ante la traición, la mentira e

indiferencia de tus amigos.
A tu sombra, niño hermoso, sigilosamente velo y sigo
tus Huellas en el camino.

Crece mi niño con cada espina,
con el esputo en tu rostro, crece;
y de cada surco de tu piel flagelada,
brote semilla de compasíon, crece fuerte.
Y cuando el dolor te ciegue, cuando los clavos
fijen tu cuerpo al frío madero y cada golpe
resuene en el cielo; cuando la hiel frunza tus labios,
y brote la vida de tu costado,
crece me niño, crece,
que aquí a tu sombra contigo lloro
y mi alma se estremece.

Retumba el cielo para acallar los gritos del alma,
la lluvia baña tu cuerpo,
mientras tu sangre pecados lava.
Y aquí están mis brazos niño, aquí está
mi pecho en llamas,
y mis labios que te cantan, arrullándote,
niño hermoso, en tu temporal morada.

Nelly Lopez
Houston, Texas

Through night air

I sing, cause my mama told me when I get scared,
sing and all the angels will echo. Hollow in a burrow,
I wait in the dark for you, where I have waited before
and will wait tomorrow, where lights cry out
like injured birds. I can see you close your office window,
and the back end of your car slides away. You can't come
to meet me anymore. I can't hear angels, no matter how long
I clamp my eyes shut, or sing you here with me.

Sarah Jefferis
Roanoke, Virginia

Life Goes On

My daughter has a favorite expression for when things go wrong: "O well, life goes on." I recently began work at a local hospital as a chaplain. Within my first week I had encountered many incidents of loss and grief. I was present at the death of an 80-year-old woman, whose family stood weeping and holding onto her and each other. Another time I attempted to offer some comfort to a couple who had given birth, only to lose the infant after one day of life.

As I attempt to process these experiences, the familiar words of my daughter take on new depth. Life does go on. For those left grieving at the bedside, life does and must go on, despite the incredible pain and loss. We believe this is also true for those who have died in our midst, albeit in a new and resurrected way. God's Spirit that was breathed into us at our *alpha* continues to breathe in us at our *omega*. And God's Spirit remains present to us in between, providing the strength, courage, power, love, comfort and sustenance to carry us through.

Our quest for spirituality—for God's Spirit—was then, is now, and will be forever. We need only tap into that eternal wellspring of life. Only then can we proclaim with joy: *"Thanks be to God. Life goes on."*

Nancy Gossling
Sandy Hook, Connecticut

Transformation

Fall

Shafts of sunlight streaming
Through autumn's arboreal splendor
Drawing us upwards along that path of light
Through nature's stained glass window

flight.

ward

ven-

Hea-

Frieda D. Carstens
Rolla, Missouri

The Stranger

A stranger knocked upon my door,
And... I let him in.
Somehow, he reminded me of you;
He was so gentle and so kind.

Quietly, he moved into my heart
And then into my soul.
It was then that I knew who
Had come to sup with me.

We broke our bread and sipped the wine
In the scented candle light.
Then, he placed his hand in mine,
And begged me go with him.

"It's not very far," he said.
"I'll go with you," was my reply.
"But, grant me one more breath," I said,
"With which to die."

Elaine Strong Skill
Vancouver, Washington

the new heaven

I want to travel like an electric pulse
across the pale lips of the lily white and down
deep into her root
exploring substance, form and ground
determining with new eyes in the darkness
how growth appears
what nutrients are called for
how to arrange resources not found
in the patterns of daily culture
and move them, readied
to flow like a muscled underground river
strong and whole and muddy
bearing the news of redemption
through the sharp crust of every arthritic tradition
that has bound us with silence to stone
laying waste old perfections
as the fingers of a new delta
plunge recklessly into the luscious
mothering depths of an oceanic matrix
creative, wild, dangerous

Peggy Hill
Kittery, Maine

Eucharist

Before the altar table stands the priest;
Her hands lift holy plate and brimming cup
Of change, that wondrous change that is the feast,
The bread and wine, the mystery held up.

Invited, I approach and drink and eat,
Forgiven, healed by love, unwrapped from fear;
Changed, fully as the bread and wine, to meet
Such love. The primal scream of change is clear.

I kneel, the outward sign is discerned. Not known
Yet sensed, the inward grace of what will be.
As bread and wine is changed, creation grows
In wondrous, varied image, changing me.

Oh Lover of my Soul, as you come near,
The touch of change has happened to me here.

Janet Lloyd
Bellevue, Washington

Chrysalis

Christ-centering,
Into Chrysalis
I move
To grow, swiftly
Becoming new
    again
In Christ.

Eleanor Smith
Tulsa, Oklahoma

A Woman's Burdens

There she is, staring back at me
   in the mirror
The woman that I am, and the
   woman that I am not.

I'm tired of reaching, Lord.
   Tired of reaching and striving
For that point of perfection
   That doesn't even exist in this life.

I am what You made me,
   And what my parents made me,
What I made me, what the world made me.
   Or am I?

Must I flow in and out of life
   Being alternately happy and sad?
Compassionate and angry? Calm and explosive?
   I feel like a neon light with a blown fuse.

Life seems too big, Lord
   And I feel so small.
My efforts leave me
   Tired and cross.

The cross?
    I've considered the cross.
It reminds me of an intersection.
Life seems to be one intersection
    after another.
A never ending series of stop and go.

But the hymn says,
    "The Way of the Cross Leads Home."
If only I could be sure.

Have faith, you say?
    Oh yes! I have it here somewhere.
Sometimes I misplace it, like my car keys.
    You know how unorganized I am.

Well, yes, I guess I did entrust
    My heart with your love.
Are you telling me the two abide together?
    Are you sure? I guess you ought to know.

Growing is painful, Lord.
    Why can't I emerge
A radiant, full-grown Christian
    Without all the bumps and potholes in the road?

The best roads to travel
 are the expressways.
Yet I know I must travel the same foot-worn path
All the other pilgrims have trod, with all its
 Crossings, with all its joys and sadness.

Forgive me, Lord, for complaining.
 The burden of being human is heavy at times.
I'd forgotten that you sent your Son
 To carry our burdens for us.

Teach me, Lord, to lay my burdens at your feet.
That I may live in your mercy so tender and sweet.

"Go forth in faith and love
 And your needs shall be met."
Help me Lord, that this promise
 I shall never forget.

Yvonne Osborn
Shreveport, Louisiana

Some Rambling Thoughts On A Spring Afternoon

D.E.M.

Crawling around on my hands and knees in my garden, I thought and meditated on a number of things. I marveled at the miracle of rebirth as one by one I found my favorite perennials and gently removed the debris that had covered them during the frozen days of winter. What joy I felt as I anticipated the brilliant colors the nine varieties of day lilies would provide from June to September.

When I came to the iris bed, I paused for awhile and thought about their endurance. Some of the iris go back to my childhood: I wondered how many times they had been separated and transplanted from one house to another as my parents or I moved. I thought about how God's love has endured over the years and the difference that love has made in so many lives. My heart soared. Occasionally, I would burst into song (off key, of course).

Mostly though, as I worked in the garden, I gave thanks to God for life: for my life, for the lives of my loved ones and for the life of Jesus Christ. I gave thanks that God loved us so much that God sent Jesus Christ that we might have eternal life. I gave thanks for being part of the Body of Christ, for the privilege of serving God and for the joys of rebirth in my garden.

Marjorie A. Burke
Lexington, Massachusetts

97

Witness

Witness

Mother Teresa

She is indeed His hands, His feet,
His voice to so many—those
Who have never known Him personally
Have glimpsed His presence in a lowly
Nun—A love that shines forth
Mid the poverty and ugliness of
people in distress. It is a light
That will not be extinguished.
Our God still comes in unexpected
Guise. He comes to people who seem
Quite bereft of decent care
And hope, to die in peace. She
Is indeed that angel unaware,
And yet to many is His very
Image, showing His love, and freely giving.
Making life, death "Something beautiful for God."
In this small nun, an inner vision dwells,
That she in turn sees Christ, the suffering One.
And grace abounds where love reciprocates,
For she has touched and loved the Christ in them.

Margery E. Harper
Bellevue, Washington

Love

Love was born in a baby...
Loves dies on a cross...
so that Love could be
born in the hearts of men and women.
New life came when one life was given.
What cost to God
His love for humankind!
What cost to us, when we see others
with Jesus' eyes of love.
What cost to me
when I respond to His love?
New Birth! New Life! New Love!
Praise the Lord!

Florence Mayer
Lexington, Kentucky

@ Home

First cold night
idle complaints
before slipping into a warm bed

Passing memory
of a man in a doorway
on a trip to the City

Bundled to obesity
reclining in a door frame
isolated by choice and head lice

I thought I walked by
clutching my bag and the throat
of my camel hair coat

But tonight I wonder
Do I have anything he wants?
Does he have something I need?

Beverly Pyle
Bethel, Connecticut

Spiritual Journey

The elementary school where I work has a food drive in early November that delivers food baskets to 20 to 40 needy families in our community. When I deliver the baskets, I am always humbled when the ladies tell me that I must be an angel from heaven. I wish I knew what to answer, but I always just say "Thank you." (I have always believed that women are angels—think of the miracle of childbirth.)

But sometimes we forget about the blessings that surround us. I remember taking a basket to a family last year. Tears running down her face, the mother sadly told me to keep the turkey because she did not have a stove. She shook her head when her children asked if they could build a fire outside. Then and there, without realizing what I was saying, I offered to cook the turkey, inviting them to dinner at my home. I will never forget the children's shouts of joy.

Recalling the day's events, I really don't know what made me open my house and my family to people I really don't know. Yet when we saw the look on their faces as we welcomed them into our kitchen, all I could do was say: "Thank you, God."

I am on a long spiritual journey, which often leads me to places where I can help—can offer what little I have. Where is your spiritual journey leading you?

Esther Reynosa
San Antonio, Texas

Orrene Raby

New Life

"Do not mistreat an alien or oppress him, for you were aliens in Egypt." —Exodus 22:21

Eagerly I open the door of an old, faded green house that is home to Hmong refugees living in our city. Each week I visit the Thaos, a family I am proud to sponsor in this country.

When I first met Joua Thor—their nephew—four years ago, he was a student in my public school class. His mother wanted to study English, so I became her tutor. As our friendship grew, the family asked me to sponsor relatives living in Thailand who wanted to come to the United States. (Because of their involvement in the Vietnam War—the Hmong fought against the Communists and rescued downed American pilots—a campaign of genocide was conducted against them as soon as Laos fell.)

Being a sponsor was much easier than anticipated, since the Thor family helped with finding a home, schools and services for their cousins. How do I continue to help them? Just being an honest friend in a foreign land is the best I have to offer. I try to teach everyday vocabulary and basic mathematics. I work from their school books and notes. They say we Americans speak so fast. Both of the Thao parents attend classes at the local technical intitute.

When we discuss life in Laos, there is deep sadness. All Hmong traveled at great risk to reach Thailand where refugee camps were set up.

I hired Boua, the father, to help rake my yard last year. After working hard for four hours, he refused to take the money I handed him. "This time I work to say thanks for your help to my family."

It brought home a point I had overlooked in our relationship: how his own self-esteem and personal worth had suffered in the refugee condition. The Hmong, like all refugees, need help to navigate the complex web of services, regulations, and cultural norms. But most of all, they need our Christian love.

Orrene Raby
Oshkosh, Wisconsin

Unity in Diversity

Unity in Diversity
The New Millennium is Ours
Break the silence
Commonality discovered
Women hold up half the sky
Keep on moving forward—never turning back
Challenges to women are universal and global
Sisterhood
Solidarity
March for Peace, Vigil for Hope

Elizabeth Hobbs
Pittsburgh, Pennsylvania

Gill England,
courtesy of The Mother's Union

A Prayer for Beyond Beijing

O God, Creator of the heavens and the earth, as those who attended the UN Fourth World Conference on Women continue their servanthood, may they know they are sisters and ambassadors for You, the "One Over All." Help all to listen for and to answer Your call for action in bringing about Your justice and equality everywhere. May the work to fulfill Your purpose become more defined each day from now until we are called to be in Your eternal Kingdom.

Amen.

Elizabeth Hobbs
Pittsburgh, Pennsylvania

The Girl at the Bus Stop

Among my many blessings, I have always given thanks for my neighbors; since starting my morning walks in my subdivision, I have come to appreciate even more the friendliness and decency of those who live nearby.

A troubling scene, however, is played out each morning on a corner I pass. The second lap of my daybreak stroll takes me past a foursome of junior high girls waiting for their school bus. They seem to be a delightful group, with all the giggles and outbursts typical of the age—until, that is, the final rider approaches the bus stop.

A fifth girl—who happens to be black—walks to the driveway at the very last moment, just ahead of the bus. The reason for her hesitation is clear, for at her approach, the others turn their backs and make a tight circle, chattering away while completely ignoring her presence. A tall hedge borders the drive, and the interloper usually waits behind it, out of view of her home a few doors away—perhaps so she will not have to explain to her parents why no one will speak to her.

My heart breaks for her every time I pass, and I wonder what her day must be like with such a grim start. I pray that she is greeted by a compassionate teacher and a band of friends when she gets to class, but I cannot be sure. What, I wonder, can I do for this child who seems so quiet, so dignified, and so totally rejected?

When I cross her path before she reaches her classmates, I always give her my best "Good morning" and some comment about the weather, exams, or praise for her new hairdo. I find myself mentally sending her on her way for a terrific day as I hear the bus grind away behind me.

I worry on the days this shy child is missing. Is she sick today? Has some meanness on yesterday's ride made her beg her parents to drive her to class this time? If I asked the other girls where their friend is, what would they answer? Most of all, I wish there were something I could say to the tight little foursome that would help; but so far nothing suitable has come to me. For now it has to be a greeting and a prayer.

In Gail Godwin's *Father Melancholy's Daughter*, there is a wonderful blessing used by Father Gower on Maundy Thursday as he blesses an outdoor crucifix marred by vandals. It is also a petition for the rejected child at the bus stop, for the clannish foursome, and for the walker who prays for them all. It is the prayer of faithful Christians who struggle with the challenge and promise of the query, "Who is my neighbor?" As we reflect on the injustice of racism, it becomes our prayer:

"Lord who on Maundy Thursday did say to Thy disciples, 'This is my body, broken for you,' permit us to use this occasion to offer Thee all our broken body parts. We ask Thee to take our broken dreams, our broken promises—promises we made to others and to ourselves. Take the broken bodies of some of us, and the broken hearts of us all. And take unto Thee everything about us we may not know is broken, and make all things whole again in Thy self."
Amen.

Catherine M. Wedding
Amarillo, Texas

Seasons

Advent Visitation

Even from the cabin window I sensed the wind's
contagion begin to infect the rags of leaves.
The alders gilded to it, obeisant, the way

angels are said to bow, covering their faces with
their wings, not solemn, as we suppose, but
possessed of a sudden, surreptitious hilarity.

When the little satin wind arrived
I felt its slide through the cracked-open door,
(a wisp of prescience? a change in the
weather?)

and after the small push of breath—You
entering with your air of radiant surprise;
I the astonished one.

These still December mornings
I fancy I live in a clear envelope of angels
like a cellophane womb. Or a soap bubble,

the colors drifting, curling. Outside
everything's tinted rose, grape, turquoise,
silver—the stones by the path, the skin of sun

on the pond ice, at night the aureola of
a pregnant moon, like me, iridescent,
almost full term with light.

Luci Shaw
Menlo Park, California

Advent Visitation

Reflections on John the Baptist

Not Neat, Not Neighborly, Not Nice
Unkempt, Uncouth, Uncivilized
Disheveled, Disruptive, Disturbing
Obnoxious, Obstreperous, Obstinate
Insulting, Insubordinate, Insolent
Tactless, Terse, Tempestuous
Riff-Raff, Rabble-Rouser, Rebel
Thorn in the side, Pain in the neck,
Dissident, Dissonant
Rude, Crude
Wild, Weird
Leftist, Baptist
A voice crying in the wilderness
A voice crying in My wilderness
(Overwhelmed, Overworked, Underloved)
You are my Conscience,
You are my Courage,
You will lead me to Christ.

LeeAnn Larson Lafave
Sioux Falls, South Dakota

Adapted from a longer version published in *Radical Grace* (August-September 1991), Center for Action and Contemplation, Albuquerque, NM.

The Annunciation of Our Lord

"And when she saw him, she was troubled at his saying, and cast in her mind what manner of salutation this should be." Luke 1:29

When preachers commend Mary for her acceptance of the Annunciation, I get uneasy lest we "damn with faint praise" an act that required more courage of Mary than will probably ever be required of any of us.

Although living faithfully requires courage in many ways, our circumstances seldom require courage of the dramatically death-defying sort. Yet Mary's circumstances required precisely that. Where Mary came from, betrothed women found pregnant got stoned to death, crushed beneath the politics of purity. Or faced a living death. In Mary's time and place, a woman's sexual intactness was her entire worth. To forfeit that worth would not only end any envisioned life with Joseph, but kill any chance of living with honor.

I imagine she was terrified. She assented anyway.

That scene makes me think of Gethsemane. Jesus here is "deeply distressed and troubled," just as Mary was "greatly troubled" at the angel's words. Jesus, bowed to the ground in anguish, prays to be spared. (He prefaces his prayer, "Everything is possible with you." Where have we heard that before?) "Take this cup from me," Jesus prays. "Yet not what I will, but what you will."

Surely this is the gospel story's moment of truth—here where Jesus could still just walk away, could so easily just slip into the night. Surely this is the moment of greatest courage, this "Yet not what I will, but what you will."

And I think, "Yes," his mother taught him everything he knew.

Lauren Glen Dunlap
Seattle, Washington

Excerpted from an essay in *Passages*, St. Paul's, Seattle.

Hail Mary

Hey Mary!
May I use a line
From your scenario?

I want to tell the world
That I am full of Grace,
A blessed woman,
Bearing to the world
A gift from God:
The Love of God
As He has given it to me.

My own annunciation,
Alleluia!

Joyce Cleave Gibb
Ellensburg, Washington

Nativity

a nest for the swallows
  a den for the fox
a pillow for Jesus
  a bed in a box
of cardboard folded on the street
  days go by when he doesn't eat
the cold winds blow
  the dark nights, too
are a part of life
  that I never knew
disciples aplenty he has, and more;
  authorities pounding on the door
and saying, "Hey you! Let's move it! Go
on!"

He opens his arms
  to take them along
to join all the saints
  in a wonderful song
of love and praise
  and laughter and joy—
the swallows, the foxes,
  and a new baby boy
who lay in a manger
  filled with straw
the cardboard box of His day.

Nancy Millat
Dayton, Ohio

116

Christmas Transformation

How glorious the fabric of warmth and love
  that transforms all on Christmas day!
A touch of the kingdom that restores the heart
  seeking to travel his heavenly way.
Yet bleak and cold and lonely can be
the soul's deep, dark, wintry night—
But is this not when the star appears,
piercing, pulsating, shimmering, bright?
Will we choose to give up inner deafness, and
  the blindness that blocks us time and time again?
And to lay down the spiritual crutches, so
  we can walk to our own Bethlehem?
There to rediscover the Christ, the Word of God,
  the vast treasure at life's very own core—
And from there shout in celebration of Christmas,
  as we have never been able to before!

Harriet Chandlee Caldwell
Lookout Mountain, Tennessee

From *A Generation of Christmas in the Words and Images of Harriet Chandlee Caldwell*

To Prepare

Be merciful to acquaint
   plenteous multitudes with Hope.
Mist of Morning's Joy echoes
   in fading haze of life's busy
Archipelago.
   Horizons dawn with risen Sun
Incurring the wondrous Presence
   of disposing dew, while sharp light
trails on refuge to prepare Him room.

Cathy Silcock
Columbia, Missouri

Ash Wednesday

On Lent's threshold
I begin to release
Old joys
And triumphs
To the heap
Of ashes
Where
My struggling faith
Can begin
To rise
Making
Gray Crosses
In remembrance
of the expenditure
Of love.

Marj Denniston
Coeur d'Alene, Idaho

The 8th Day of Lent, 1981
(with apologies to T.S. Eliot)

Oh Lord: take our minds and think through them
        take our lips and speak through them
        take our hearts and set them on fire

blessed Litany for living

Oh Lord: to my prayer on Tuesday

        To cancel my blindered one-way passage, cataracts
        To See....out of others' eyes
        To Hear....out of others' silences
        To Share.....out of others' pain
        To Give....out of others' needs
        To Love and Respond

Empty-handed, and with tears, to that petition and repentance
Thy Spirit gave the long-sought grace of gentleness

        From Calvary of concentricity
        To Tenderness transfigured
        My Life's crossroads to caring.

Why did it take me so long,
While thy gift was given overnight?

Oh Lord: grant that gentleness abide with me.

Louise Butler Uhl
Norfolk, Virginia

119

Holy Week

"Mary took a pound of costly ointment of pure nard and anointed the feet of Jesus and wiped his feet with her hair..." John 12:1-11

What a personal, intimate scene in our Lord's life with which we begin our observance of Holy Week. It is easy for most of us to identify with Martha, busily preparing and serving a meal, and with Judas and others who criticize Mary for wasting a precious commodity.

Yet Mary is difficult for many of us. Is it because what she does is too personal, too intimate? Is it because it is too risky? Or, is it because in our own culture we are unwilling to give up our costly ointment called Time to offer at the feet of our Lord?

Penny Sisson
Oxford, Mississippi

Of Lists and Lent

How do you observe Lent? I believe there are two distinct ways of observing this holy season. If you are orderly, make lists and have a neat office or home you do it one way. If you put stuff down anywhere, and juggle five tasks at once, then Lent becomes something else.

We tend either to add things to life in Lent or take them away, go to mid-week services or not eat dessert, read an extra holy book or not see a movie. The orderly person ticks off a list of deeds; giving up something is a once and all decision. No smoking, no desserts, no alcohol in Lent. I can remember that first taste of wine at Easter Sunday brunch.

The other type of person just hopes that their Lent is bringing them closer to God. Sure they attend mid-week services, and read and pray, but Lent is more a holistic experience. But no fighting with one's husband, or being kind to a co-worker is a continuous struggle; there's no ticking off of lists here. For me, I find that being intentional about my relationship with God and his other children—for at least forty days a year—is more meaningful.

Where do you fall on this continuum?

Jenny Ladefoged
Los Angeles, California

Of Lists and Lent

Learning to Make Easter Bread

She cups her left hand
holds cardamon, anise seeds
fragile saffron threads
while her right hand sprinkles
brandy and wine over yeast.
She asks if I understand
the meaning of spices, wine
I say yes of course
anxious to record ingredients.
I don't understand
this old woman who listens
to Puccini, wears black stockings
and aprons, covers her head
with cotton scarves
tied at the nape of her neck.

She crosses herself
when the dough doubles
lifts it onto a board
caresses in circles
divides and holds up
three swinging strands.
She braids and makes them one.
I nod, I have everything

written down, no need to stay.
At dawn I hear
Puccini's The Swallow
and her voice.
Che Importa la ricchezza
se alfin e rifiorita la felicita?
What do riches matter
compared with happiness in full flower?
Must she sing Puccini on Easter?
Dishes rattle in the china cabinet.
I think she's dancing, dancing!
I try to make bread
for this full-moon feast
but something is missing—
lemon balm, rose geraniums in pots
fragrance from her kitchen garden?
How many years will it take
how many do I have,
to learn to sing Puccini
and to dance, to dance?

Patricia Flower Vermillion
Hampton, Virginia

Easter Vigil

The song of Easter
began in me
long before memory,
a child's understanding
of love,
without asking or seeking—
given, like a hum
on the lips. Not knowing
where it came from,
the song, hummed, sung,
breaking like a full-orchestrated
melody over my whole life.
My God, singing I love
your love, your Word, your
endless, rapturous song of Life.
Singing, I am sung.

Joal Harris Donovan
Galveston, Texas

Variation 2

Lord, we come humbly on this Easter Eve
full of our own preparations—
Knowing only you can give us the divine requirement.
We stand now as empty vessels in these silent moments
and pray for you to fill us with your Holy Spirit,
so that as we dare to catch and impart your light tonight,
We may do so burning with the living flame of your love.
Amen.

Shirley Wilson
Newport News, Virginia

Cecelia Dalzell

Joy

Spring's Daffodils are joy
Unto themselves:

A spot of sheer
Tranquility,

Their sunshine trumpets
Silently

Of Resurrection Day!

Patsy F. LaVallee
Danbury, Connecticut

Ascension

Make me Thy captive even as the raging sea.
What if my waves are restless like its own,
Forever pounding an unchanging shore,
Forever bounded yet forever free?
I live, and yet I do not live alone,
I live and ever love Thee more and more.
Thou, Who didst bid the raging waves be still,
Speak to my heart and bind me to Thy will.

Free me from all that holds me fast to earth,
Those false entanglements that lure me back
From the divine captivity of Thy will,
Those fleshly pleasures that even from my birth
Clung to my life and made my will grow slack.
Make me Thy captive on Thy Holy Hill,
And lift me as a wave upon the sea
That I, Thy prisoner, may at last be free.

Sister Catherine Louise
Boston, Massachusetts

Barbara Mallonee

The Green Season

Leaves of a green that pulses,
Deep, heavy, complete;
A shade bespeaking peak and prime,
Full, pendulous, bursting;
Completion and expectation suspended.

Fulfillment of Easter and Pentecost are past;
Expectancy of Advent is distant;
And the weeks between hold us
In lazy summer heat
Before the blazing, the bareness that follows:
In the quest for healing, hoping;
In our love, and our thrust toward God.

Catherine M. Wedding
Amarillo, Texas

Collect and Reflection on All Saint's Day

Creator Mother, who has set the moon among
us to bring light in darkness: bring us evermore to
turn our whole beings toward you, that the gift of
our incarnation may shine on all who perish for
want of a reflection of you, that we may ever
glorify him who is that Bright and Morning Star.
Amen.

Becky Niemeyer
Denver, Colorado

Communion of Saints

When we are orphaned
Bereft of parents
Or as we orphan ourselves
We allow them
To live on in us
As we gradually assimilate
Their God-given qualities
Of goodness
And we and they
Become part of
The communion of saints
As we die unto self
And move into
An awakening
Of Christ's Spirit.

Marj Denniston
Coeur D'alene, Idaho

All Saints

In a bitter season, in rained air and the sharp
Scent of leaves, the brewed tea of November
Invites what hushes reasoning. It is a region of
Soul, tattered and nothing new, an old, old weather
Keeping account with the earth's remorseless mood.
All the departed gather. They are aerial, brushing
Like wind, taking no shape. In a fading year
Color succumbs, days turn under. The numbing
grey
Becomes a sudden window. They are here,
affirming,
Letting the light pass through, proving the eternal.

Erin Wells
Charlottesville, Virginia